I0485146

Dead or Alive

The use and relevance of the Deadpan
aesthetic in contemporary photographic
portraiture.

Robin Austen

Dead or Alive

Copyright © 2019 Robin Austen

All rights reserved.

ISBN: 9781072462927

DEDICATION

For my Wife and Son. For my Mother and Father.
For my Sister. And most importantly, for Myself.

Dead or Alive

In recent years there has been a growing popularity within photographic portraiture (especially that within the fine art realm) that subscribes to an ever more blank and confusing mode of photographic approach. The Deadpan aesthetic that has become so prevalent and 'valued' in this area of practice has been the source of much debate, and at times, frustration.

In order to understand this approach better, this piece of writing briefly outlines the use of the Deadpan aesthetic in contemporary photography within this area. It attempts to roughly define this aesthetic and assess its relevance within this genre of photographic practice by investigating its use, and analyzing its effect in important artworks from its origins to the present day. It makes indirect comparisons between these works, using key theorists and theories to evaluate its place within modern day image making.

The most commonly used (and arguably most accurate) definition of the Deadpan aesthetic, is proposed by Charlotte Cotton, remarking that Deadpan is "a cool, detached and keenly sharp type of photography" (Cotton, 2009 p105). Her definition implies an image state devoid of drama or emotional recourse, which takes an objective and 'factual' standpoint to its subject. In the case of portraiture, this comes in the form of a blank, emotionless gaze straight down the lens, with little to no visual cues, and often flatly lit. It is said that this approach is a "return to documentary values in contemporary photography." (Smee, 2003); however, this is not from where Deadpan originated.

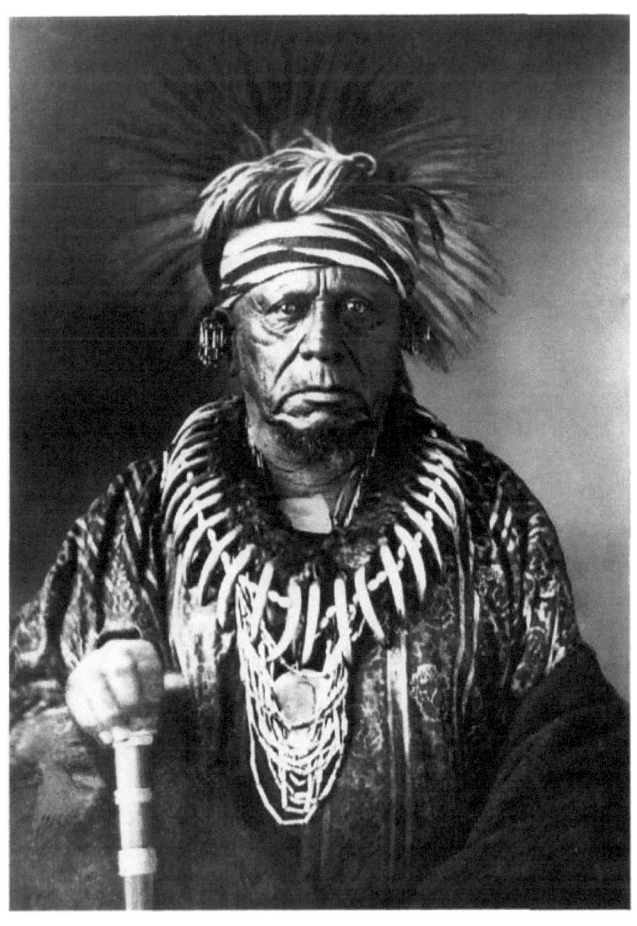

Fig 1. Thomas Easterly, 1847, Keokuk Sauk Chief

Although the term 'Deadpan' was not introduced until much later in order to describe the aesthetic, the first instances of this within photographic portraiture can be seen in examples from photography's youth, as "smiling for a photograph didn't become commonplace until the 1880s, when roll film and faster cameras made it possible to capture more spontaneous expressions." (Coleman, 2013). The limitations of the early large format equipment, required sitters to remain still for many minutes, and thus adopting an expression that was easy to hold for this length of time was common, and was quintessentially what we now describe as to be Deadpan.

As photographic technology improved in the years following this point, expressive and spontaneous imagery became the more prevalent and preferred mode of photographic approach for many.

However, in the early to mid 1900's, the work of the Bechers brought Deadpan back from the grave in a new way.

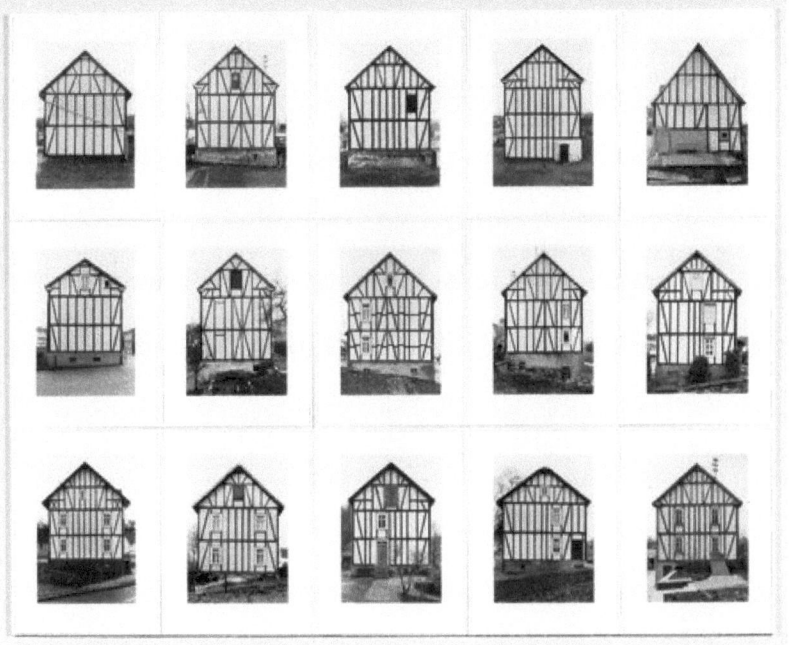

Fig 2. Bernd and Hilla Becher, 1959-71, Framework houses

Although speculated that their work was partially a product of the strict Nazi regulations against expressive artwork in Germany at the time, it is apparent that "the photographic world of the Bechers is committed to *objectivity*" (Costello and Iversen, 2010 p51). By taking a systematic approach to their image making process (by taking all of their photographs in/at similar weather, light, height, distance etc.) they were able to create "a mode of photography that is emotionally detached or 'neutral' in the sense that it does not make outright judgments, and thus tends to emphasize what might be called an 'evidentiary' condition" (Costello and Iversen, 2010 p30).

This mode of photography, although an 'objective' approach, does so only in an attempt to remove the subjectivity of the photographer as an expressive agent, achieving this through its formal representation of a subject, assuming no personal connection or history to it, allowing its factuality to become present, and for the subject to tell its own story. Through this "the Bechers' work can be understood as 'embodied expression'...as it attempts to objectify without reification, to express without expressing something." (Costello and Iversen, 2010 p64).

It is this quality and way of thinking that was passed from the Bechers to their students, who now form what we commonly call the 'Dusseldorf school' of photography. One of the most prolific photographers in this 'school' was Thomas Ruff.

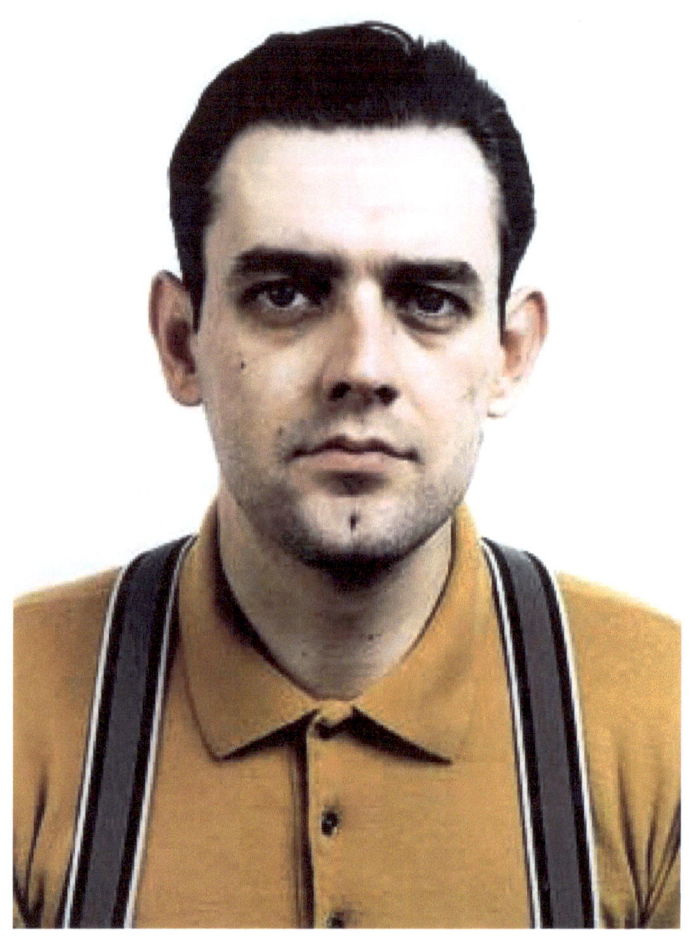

Fig 3. Thomas Ruff, 1986, Portrait 1986 (Stoya)

Taking the teachings of the Bechers and applying them to his portraiture, Ruff worked in a similarly meticulous fashion, taking images at a similar distance, with the same large format equipment, in equally unflattering light, always with a blank expression in a common 'head and shoulders' passport style.

Although his portraits were taken as a reaction to the government's obsessive identity checks, in response to the 'Red Army Faction' terrorist group attacks at the time, Ruff's work had a much more profound and far-reaching affect. His work questions absolutely the pre-conception of photographic identity, as "the works blank expressions and lack of visual triggers, such as gesture, confound our expectations of discovering a person's character through their appearance (Cotton, 2009 p106) and "Ruff's objectively styled pictures dramatically curtail our expectations that we can know anything essential about a person through their photographic image." (Cotton, 2009 p107).

This raises the issue of photographic authenticity and the truthfulness of the subject's portrayal, and our understanding of our ability to really 'know' anything about the subject based on a photographic representation of it. By removing all social or visual cues in these images, the viewer is not restricted in their questioning of the individual within the image. Instead, every aspect of character is questioned. The image serves purely as a record of being, through which the subject tells its own story.

By taking this objective approach, it could be understood that comments are made on the way in which we view and judge others through the clinical assessment of body language, appearance and the use of self-presentation, whereby "every gesture and expression is a form of social currency." (Coleman, 2013).

This idea was also pushed in a different direction, which questions "If there are realities or truths held within the deadpan portrait, they revolve around the very subtle signs of how people react to being photographed" (Cotton, 2009 p107), which is a key theme by another of the Becher's students, Rineke Dijkstra.

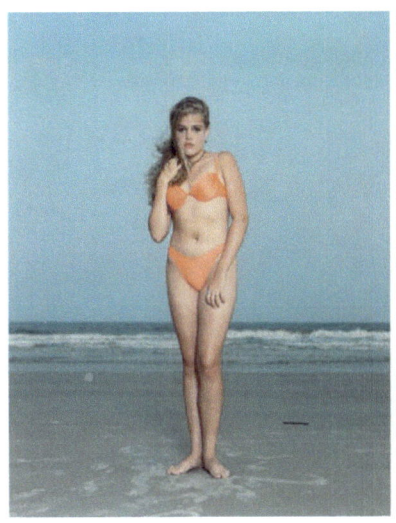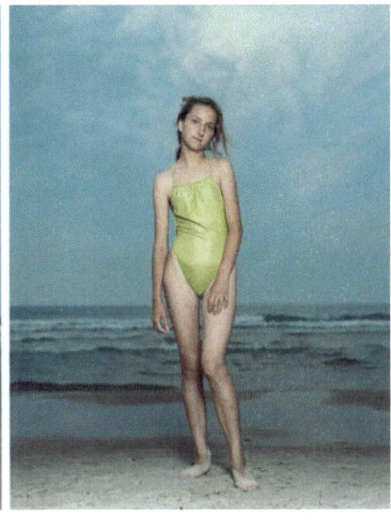

Fig 4. Rineke Dijkstra, 1992, Hilton Head Island, S.C., USA, June 24, 1992

Fig 5. Rineke Dijkstra, 1992, Kolobrzeg, Poland, July 26, 1992

Her work is said to take "The unsentimental approach" (Cotton, 2009 p112) to the subject in hand. Most famously evident in her 'Beaches' series, where similarly to Ruff's work ethic, a standardized framework of image making was employed.

Shooting ritualistically from the same height and angle, using the same equipment, a comparative body of images was produced, focusing on a specific moment where adolescents are caught in their bathing suits between the protection of their emersion in the sea, and the anonymity of clothing on land.

Through doing this "Dijkstra captured the vulnerability and physical self-consciousness of her subjects" (Cotton, 2009 p112), in a way that may not have been apparent or demonstrated through any other means, allowing personal style and stance to be viewed through the subject's reaction to the act of being photographed. As

Dijkstra repeatedly stresses the solitary character of her subjects and says that she wants to get at the essential, human aspect of them. By apparently stripping away the social, in focusing on circumstances where its hold seems shakiest, she seeks to reveal the essentially human. (Stallabrass, 2007).

Interestingly, unlike Ruff, Dijkstra trades the unflattering lighting for external flashes in this body of work. The result is an effect where the subject appears 'cut-out' and 'removed' from the background. The use of this combined with the Deadpan approach parodies the aesthetic of fashion imagery, and implies a disconnection from social surroundings in individuals that are yet to fully understand, engage or be affected by this industry. This effect also distances and distills the subject into a 'silenced' state of being that canonizes the individual, turning them into spectacle. The use of this ethnographic stance was previously criticized for creating the separation of the 'other' within sub-cultures from its use in documentary photography. However, by utilizing this process and turning it onto her own social class, this is avoided, and it is possible to speculate that in doing so, Dijkstra is able to effectively represent the instability of individuality and identity within society at the time, making comments on the ever growing power of mass consumerism and popular culture.

Other than just creating a comparative record of the reaction to the act of being photographed, and the self-presentation within the subjects during this process, the approach taken also allows her to retain the essence of subject through an objective process.

If this approach had not been employed, it would not have been demonstrated that "Such images oscillate between identification and distancing, honoring and belittling, critical recognition and the enjoyment of spectacle, and access to the real and the critique of realist representation." (Stallabrass, 2007).

As Dijkstra's 'Beaches' series briefly comments, this Deadpan approach has become popularized and reabsorbed into mainstream culture through its use in fashion and lifestyle imagery. This was pushed into public view by many, but none more so than by Richard Avedon. Although by this point he was already a successful and established photographer, it was the creation of his influential series 'In the American West' that caused most controversy, debate and awareness of this mode of image making within the public eye.

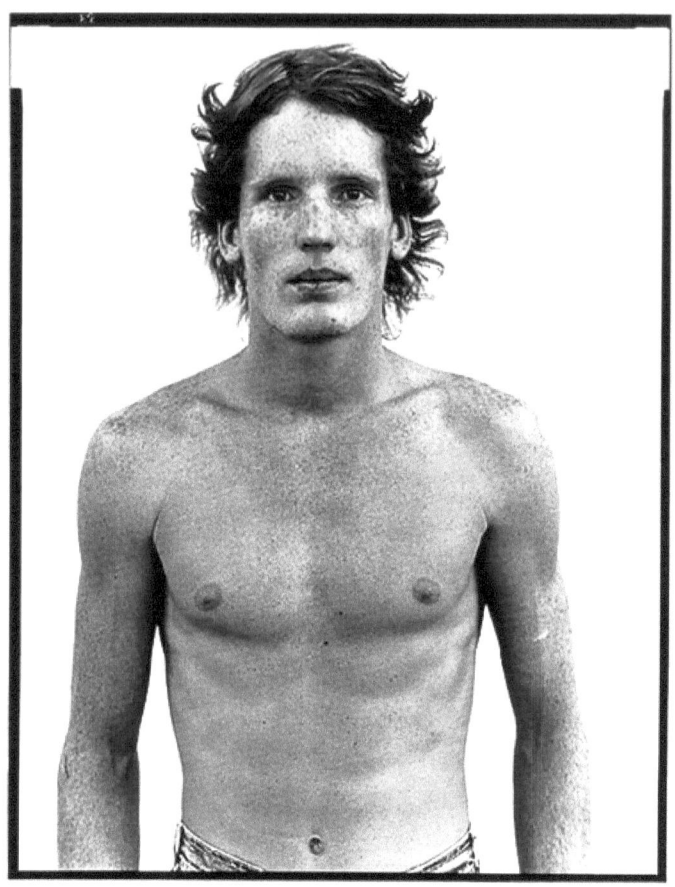

Fig 6. Richard Avedon, 1983, Jay Greene, Grain Thresher

Avedon's series was a commission to photograph the people of the American west; however, upon completion, his work caused outrage. By using the

Deadpan approach, and many of the ideas first presented in the work of the Beecher's, Ruff and Dijkstra, he gave a frank portrayal of those that occupied the American west, shunning the expected romanticized notion of them held by many, and criticized for belittling and misrepresenting the people of the area.

By taking his subject's out of context from their surroundings, the impact of living in this region on the individual can be seen. Like Ruff's series, in this sterile environment we question our preconceptions of knowledge about the individual and our romantic notions of such, and through their own self presentation and reaction to the act of being photographed (similar to those in Dijkstra's work) the subject is given the ability to tell their own individual story through the conveyance of 'nothing at all'.

It was the reaction to this body of work, and the perceived 'truthfulness' of the images that led to another commission for Avedon, shooting commercial fashion advertising work for Levi's in the same approach as 'In the American West'. This became an extremely successful advertising campaign, resonating strongly with the 'everyday' masses, and the deadpan aesthetic was quickly adopted by many other major brands for advertising use.

Although this in itself does not bring much of anything new to the table in photographic terms, it drew attention to the power of the aesthetic, and not only just through the 'truthful' aspect that it has been said to express. It also sparked closer examination and debate as to the gaze employed by the subjects within his work, and other works created in this same mode.

Frequently described as bored, emotionless and blank, the gazes in these images are far from immensely expressive, however there is much more to that which meets the eye. Besides merely fixing and directly connecting with a viewer, they are the epitome of 'indifference'. It marks the understanding that this state of emotional or expressive 'being' is perhaps not a state of emotionlessness, but an expressive state of its own that is simply devoid of both any positive or negative emotional recourse. It can be seen as a base line from which the ability to show other forms of emotional expression stem from, as our "understanding of being is to begin with indifference" (Costello and Iversen, 2010:40) and it is a way of "opening us to the 'nothingness', 'abyss' or 'void' of being" (Costello and Iversen, 2010 p41).

In terms of the success and popularization of the Deadpan aesthetic in fashion and advertising imagery brought about by Avedon's 'In the American West' series (and his subsequent commission by Levi's), it has not only caused further investigation into the gaze associated with this approach (which would not have been apparent if shot in a different more subjective, emotional and expressive way), but also identifies that this state of 'indifference' as the most universally natural form of being, and thus, the most accessible to viewers.

The Deadpan approach and its associated gaze essentially form what can be likened to a 'blank' canvas, whereby "As viewers, we bring our own psychological weather to the images we consume" (Coleman, 2013) through the creative act of viewing. Although this process is employed in the viewing of any visual image by a spectator, the 'accessibility' of the gaze featured through the Deadpan approach allows the subject to become an 'everyman', enabling viewers of any emotional state or line of thought to most easily relate directly to those presented within an image.

In more recent photographic works, the Deadpan approach is still present in a significant number of images, and it seems that using this aesthetic approach is still growing in both strength and popularity with a number of image-makers.

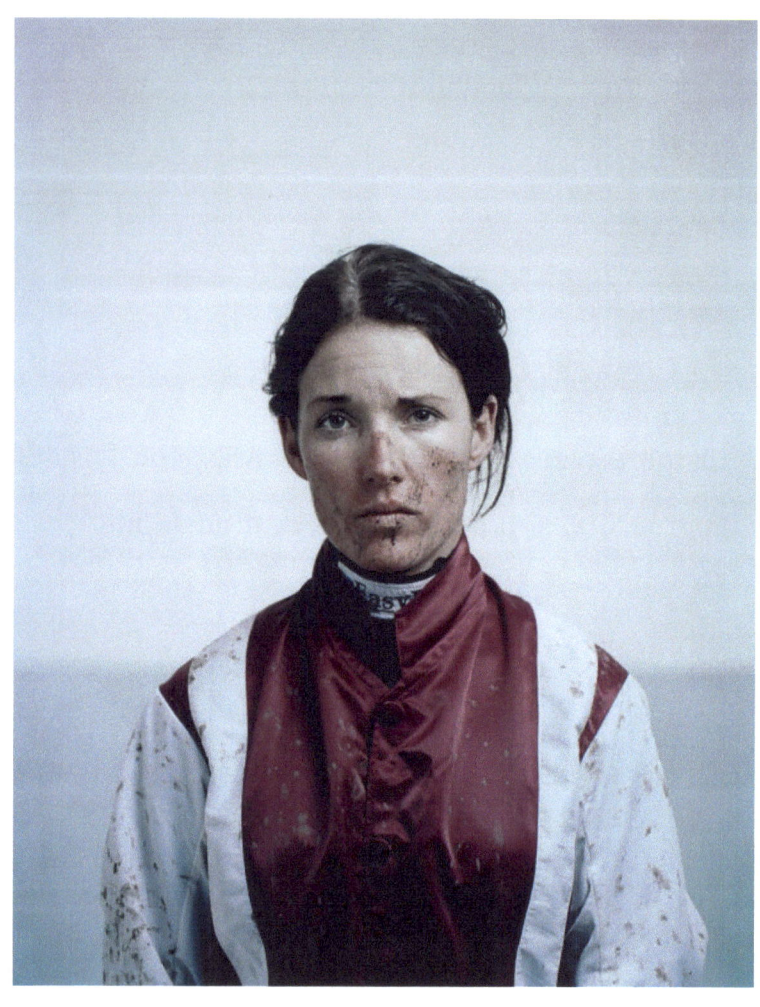

Fig 7. Spencer Murphy, 2013, Katie Walsh

For instance, take 2013's Taylor Wessing Portrait Prize winning image of jockey Katie Walsh by Spencer Murphy.

The Deadpan aesthetic is instantly recognizable, taking obvious influence from Ruff's head and shoulders style portraits, and captured at a Dijkstra-esque moment directly after disembarking from her steed. It has all the hallmarks of classic Deadpan, and this sense of distilment and 'the everyman' is exuded, choosing "to shoot the series on large format film, to give the images a depth and timelessness" (Evans, 2013).

However, unlike Dijkstra's work, rather than the awkward self-presentation and guarded reactions to the act of being photographed that we might expect to see in the subject, there is simply no notable reaction at all. Instead, we are faced with a state of almost complete passivity, even more so than those pictured in Ruff's work.

A sentiment that is now heavily present within the contemporary deadpan portraits of today.

Although, is this really any surprise? In an ever-increasing digital age, mobile technology has become a fully integrated part of our everyday modern lives. Every portable device now includes a camera, and as a result, our attitudes towards picture taking have changed dramatically over the past decade. But is that all that's happening?

The once somewhat 'punchy' imagery of early Deadpan, has now been (in most cases) punched out, and replaced with de-saturated and muted tones, creating the colour equivalent of the

Becher's Germanic, Nazi-controlled, low contrast black and whites, and carrying the same sense of melancholic oppression. It's possible to speculate that this could symbolically suggest the 'colorfulness' of life being washed out, whether this is from the current period of the most intense social, political and economic change seen in recent years, or the continuing sense of isolation and alienation felt due to the growing interconnectedness of individuals since the rise of the internet. This is just speculation of course, however, it is clear to see that this somber shift in colour and tone certainly reinforces the 'blandness' already well established within this aesthetic approach.

But, is this approach still relevant in portraiture today? And why might it be growing in such popularity?

The answers to these questions could potentially be numerous, complex, and can only really be investigated thoroughly through hindsight.

However, there are inferences to be had. We now live in a world saturated by imagery, from magazines, to online content, advertisements to television, even more so than any other generation before. As such our visual literacy has expanded at an exponential rate, allowing us to decipher ever more complex imagery at a simple glance. Could it be that the Deadpan aesthetic, through its lack of visual cues and ambiguous intentions, is able to universally engage us in a visually accessible manner, without pretense or bias, but with enough subtlety and hidden meaning that it causes us to slow down, and satisfies our growing need for increasingly challenging imagery?

One thing is clear, however. That through the cultivation of such a global and instantaneous mass media and information sharing culture, whereby we are now bombarded with facts, figures and recent events within a moment of them occurring, it could be viewed that as a society we have become beaten into a state of desensitization, indifference and overload.

The visual refinements that since its conception now empower this approach, even on a cross-cultural scale, may well reflect our newfound inability to process such a high level of constant knowledge, that is all too often infused with connotations of fear, anger, distrust and other emotional intensities. Perhaps this "detached, distant, analytical approach somehow distills our cultural mood?" (Cook, 2007), and the real reason behind the recent popularization of the Deadpan, can be explained by the aesthetics ability to provide a much-needed "refuge from emotion at a time when many of us are overwhelmed with worries about terrorism, war, ecological disaster?" (Cook, 2007).

So what can be learned about the definition of the Deadpan aesthetic from this investigation?

It can be seen that this is more than just an aesthetic trend, but a 'clinical' approach and framework to photographic production, a mode of investigation, and a prism through which any subject can be explored. Deadpan gives the ability to remove the photographer as an express agent, to question our preconceptions of being able to know anything about a subject based on a photographic representation of it. It allows us the ability to create comparative bodies of work free from bias. Allows us to identify with a subject while also canonizing it, causes the subject to become an 'everyman', distilled, timeless, and universally accessible. And it now seems that it provides an emotional shelter from an emotionally charged world.

But most importantly, the Deadpan aesthetic is an objective process, which by some feat does not objectify, but instead retains the essence of personal subjectivity by slowing us down, inviting study, and ultimately questioning.

In this context, its relevance is unquestionable. It seems we are now in an age where Deadpan fulfills our current insatiable need for challenge, identification, aspiration, and silence.

Although, this is by no means a full definition. Through its continued use further secrets of this aesthetics power are uncovered, growing our understanding of its potential and importance. It is impossible to speculate the future for Deadpan, and how its established history and cachet may be expanded. However, like all other instances, popularization may be its downfall, as many already oppose the use of this aesthetic, and call for a return to the highly personalized and expressive.

Will Deadpan continue to expand its 'valued' favorability within photographic portraiture, or will it succumb to over popularization and fall from use, reserved only for the fine arts and the highly educated? Only time will tell, after all:

"A portrait! What could be more simple and more complex, more obvious and more profound" - Charles Baudelaire – 1859.

Bibliography

Smee, S. (2003) <u>The New Passion for Deadpan</u>. [Online].
London: The Telegraph. Available from:
http://www.telegraph.co.uk/culture/art/3589720/The-new-
passion-for-deadpan.html [accessed 1 December 2013]

Cook, G. (2007) <u>Heres Looking At You</u>. [Online]. Boston:
Globe Newspaper Company. Available from:
http://www.boston.com/news/globe/living/articles/2007/11/04/he
res_looking_at_you/?page=full [accessed 20 January 2014]

Coleman, S. (2013) <u>Don't Say Cheese: Why Do the People in
Contemporary Art Photographs Look So Blank</u>. [Online]. New
York: International Association of Art Critics. Available from:
http://www.aicausa.org/news/2-articles-by-art-writing-
workshop-participant-sarah-coleman [accessed 28 November
2013]

Costello, D. and Iversen, M. (eds) (2010) Photography After Conceptual Art. Chichester: Wiley-Blackwell.

Cotton, C. (ed) (2009) The Photograph As Contemporary Art. (2nd ed.) London: Thames & Hudson.

Stallabrass, J. (2007) Whats in a Face? Blankness and Significance in Contemporary Art Photography. [Online]. Massachusetts: The MIT Press. Available from: http://www.jstor.org/discover/10.2307/40368490?uid=3738032 &uid=2478039473&uid=2134&uid=2&uid=70&uid=3&uid=60 &sid=21103282914491 [accessed 28 November 2013]

Evans, N. (2013) Spencer Murphy wins Taylor Wessing Photographic Portrait Prize 2013 for picture of jockey Katie Walsh. [Online]. London: Taylor Wessing. Available from: https://www.taylorwessing.com/news-insights/details/spencer-murphy-wins-taylor-wessing-photographic-portrait-prize-2013-for-picture-of-jockey-katie-walsh-2013-11-13.html [accessed 28 March 2014]

List of Illustrations

Fig 1. Thomas Easterly, 1847, Keokuk Sauk Chief. Available at http://www.all-art.org/history658_photography2.html (Accessed 5th December 2013 at 18:04)

Fig 2. Bernd and Hilla Becher, 1959-71, Framework houses. Available at http://www.artgallery.nsw.gov.au/collection/works/L2011.26.a-o/ (Accessed 20th December 2013 at 20:24)

Fig 3. Thomas Ruff, 1986, Portrait 1986 (Stoya). Available at http://www.tate.org.uk/art/artists/thomas-ruff-2602 (Accessed 3rd January 2014 at 10:52)

Fig 4. Rineke Dijkstra, 1992, Hilton Head Island, S.C., USA, June 24, 1992. Available at http://hyperallergic.com/57764/rineke-dijkstra-retrospective-guggenheim/ (Accessed 15th January 2014 at 13:48)

Fig 5. Rineke Dijkstra, 1992, Kolobrzeg, Poland, July 26, 1992. Available at http://hyperallergic.com/57764/rineke-dijkstra-retrospective-guggenheim/ (Accessed 15th January 2014 at 13:48)

Fig 6. Richard Avedon, 1983, Jay Greene, Grain Thresher. Available at http://www.richardavedon.com/#s=8&mi=2&pt=1&pi=10000&p=7&a=0&at=0 (Accessed 1st February 2014 at 12:37)

Fig 7. Spencer Murphy, 2013, Katie Walsh. Available at http://www.spencermurphy.co.uk/project/portfolio/ (Accessed 21st March 2014 at 22:19)

ABOUT THE AUTHOR

Robin Austen studied at Plymouth College of Art, graduating with a degree in Commercial Photgraphy, where he specialized in creative contemporary portraiture, fashion and advertising. He has since become an award winning photographer, and his work has been widely published and exhibited.

www.ingramcontent.com/pod-product-compliance
Lightning Source LLC
Chambersburg PA
CBHW040818200526
45159CB00024B/3027